Wish Weeds

Bobbi Dean

Wish Weeds
Copyright: Bobbi Dean
Published: October 2020
ISBN: 978-0-578-76029-2

Printed in the United States of America

This book was published with the assistance of Self-Publishing Relief, a division of
Writer's Relief.

Cover design by Self-Publishing Relief
© Bobbi Dean, 2020

For Bill, my biggest supporter,
who likens my smile to the poetry of flowers
and encourages me with every wish weed I put into words.

flower petals spread

open teasing bumblebees'

wings in apple trees

CONTENTS

Wish Weeds

Unstrung Pearls

Unstrung Pearls, cont'd.

Grace O'Sundays

Wish Weeds

THE WISH

Billy digs his hand
in his pocket and
takes out a penny

It is his to throw
in the wishing pool

Sandy tosses hers in
"Balloons! I want lots of balloons--
all I can get!"

Scott shouts, "Cotton Candy
for me! And I want Daddy
to read me two stories before bed!"

Billy tosses his penny in last,
the silver and copper coins
look back at him like shinny faces

Mommy asks, "What did
you wish for?"

He slips his small hand
back into hers
and answers,
"I wished I could be gooder."

HIGH WIRE ACT

driving by watching

the sparrows lift

from the telephone wire

swoop

like the hawks

they are in their

little bird dreams

coming to rest

on the grassy

meadow below

IO'S BLUSH*

The blushing Io, daughter of Inachus,
lowers her lilac lashes
    sweet upon pleasing her god--
Zeus
    the all-powerful one.

He looks a boy,
in love with the lovely

Io
    child of the River.

Forgetting stern authority within his sphere
    he bends easily
to laughter,
charmed as a school boy
    presenting first-time flowers
plucked from Eleusian Fields.

His gift,
    Spring's bird-footed violets
purpled and splashed
in yellow flecks
        mirroring
        Io's deep eyes.

Coquettishly she accepts the bouquet.

Hand in hand

        Io and Zeus walk along

the river's soft green path,

giddy as mortals in love.

*　*　*

*According to Greek legend, Zeus created the Violet
as a particularly fragrant food for Io, daughter of Inachus, the
river god.

PICKING TOMATOES

I remember my grandfather's garden.

I remember the prickly stalks of tomato plants

as I touch the leaves and stems,

reaching for the fruit.

I remember the hot new skin of a big red tomato held heavy in

my hand.

I remember Grandad sprinkling salt on my first bite.

I remember seeds and juice dripping down my chin

sticking to me.

I remember walking back to the house,

tomatoes in a paper sack.

I feel my Grandad's hand in mine,

sharing the day.

I feel loved.

SEPTEMBER'S ASTER

September's Aster
queen of outcropped meadows
bold in her subtleties
slightly bent to Autumn's breeze

reigns in lavender glory
brushed in the center with gold
sans curlicued petals
eyelash-length fringes instead

flower of simplicity
stands amongst tall
weeds of conviction
sure of her worth and sway

all the drifted days
hone her strength against
winter's clutch
offering fall's sweetest juice

just a hint of fragrance lingering
lures the bee
to her velvety bosom
free and open in her desire

SITTING ON THE BEACH IN SHOREHAM, LONG ISLAND, NEW YORK

Before my eyes I see the waves
    wash up on the shore
        then pull back in on themselves
Pebbles tumble in the surf
        turning bottle-glass into children's treasure

Behind me shoreline stretches onto beach,
        grains of sand grown hot to touch
        cool in evening foam

On the horizon the setting sun glows magenta
        against the water's surface
Before me pearly phosphorescent jellyfish
        shimmer like laughter as my hand
        reaches in for a shake

Reflections gradually return to calm
        unwrinkling cares of the day
Quiet fireflies test their lights
        blinking around me at the salty air

Occasionally a shooting star sizzles
        through August's heaven
        mirrored in the rhythm of the waves

I miss this beach more than ever

UNEVEN THREADS

The sky is not only blue,

       the uniform color of my mother-in-law's
       Wedgwood tea cup,
the perfectly-even
       flat, matte vessel
       acceptable to a few
       who drink
sip by measured sip
       starch-backed faces
tied in quiet talk
watching the clock
from high-backed Queen Anne's

The sky is not only blue,

       but spun in uneven threads of dappled
reds, oranges, yellows, greens
spilled-over
       in soft violet
       through the end-of-day window
       sneaking a peak at
village women gathered
around the lacy tablecloth
       covered in
       comfortable, chipped crockery
offering tea and cakes
for any who ask

The sky is not only blue,

       as the sun sinks,
blackening the air for night stars

above this cottage by the beach,
the white-edged doorway light

shines through the open frame,
stumbling over unmade faces
crackled in laughter
merry with gossip
giving away

one simple secret of Sisterhood

.

KADIATU

Cool air hangs in my hut from the night before. Kadiatu quietly appears. As date palms and cassava leaves sharpen in the lightening sky I see her features more clearly. First there is the smile of white, white teeth, then the soft-napped outline of her hair. She has two pink plastic curlers attached to her head. They look funny, out of place in this nearly-wild jungle clearing. The grass-roofed houses are temporary, indulged by Mother Nature. Kadiatu has cleared the overnight growth on the path to my village. She speaks simple English. We are friends.

I try not to let the concern well-up in my eyes as the morning sky brightens and the sun gains authority. The bruises on her cheek are fresh and tender. Her big, black eyes tell me, sh-h-h, this is to be expected. I am but a wife. Property, little more.

I look away busying myself with morning chores. Gourds are gathered for the day's tree-tapping. Palm juice to be collected ferments in the fuzzy heat only the equator can produce. Small hands offer the ladle. Elders expect tribute.

Kadiatu rubs bits of dry wood into flame to make a three-stoned fire. She drags a broken comb through a loosened curl and smiles. The black smoke of the cooking-fire begins to fill my hut. The morning rice must be prepared.

I am white. I am male. I am foreign. All I can do is bask quietly in her dignity, grateful she is alive.

YELLOW VIOLET

Yellow Violet in the woods

wild

uncomplicated by society's

grooming

forest leaves and needles

provide protection

enough

TWO DOVES

two doves on a wire
        do not know I watch
and smile at their cooing

wind trembles their wire
        just a bit
and they cling fast

feathers ruffle in the air
        and still they face
each other's longing

away from the crowd
        high on their wire
all below seems senseless

my heart hears their song
        as if it
were mine to own

QUEEN ANNE'S LACE

Queen Anne's Lace
carries carrot family roots
hardy vegetable fare
transformed
delicate tea-time fancy

her lacy flowered center cups
one purple tear of heart's
blood coaxed from sorrow
like a society lady
bound in stays and satin skirts
parasol over her shoulder
held in demure flattery

the lady mimics the Queen's petaled bonnet
her pulse alone
vulnerable to a hearts' loss

sad lady with a parasol
sits in the shade
sipping country lemonade
her milk white face turned
against a soft-clouded sky colored
God's blue-before-a-shower

Queen Anne's Lacey flowerets
nod and bob barely lifting
in breeze over the lady's luncheon plate
adorned in consoméed carrots
homely cousin to the flower Queen

such tiny flower faces
tickling the cut-crystal vase

hovered above the edge of her plate
society's gentle lady
fork in hand
unaware the mingled heritage
humble carrot and lacey Queen
grown together

THE ROSE DANCERS

Daughter
      stands on the threshold,
a portal her Mother passed through years ago,
      the awning heavy with red roses
dancing in the breeze,
      inside,
      Mother's hand holds
a sable paintbrush
      poised a moment in mid-air
outside,
Daughter watches
      mother-artist stand back
         critical of the slash of crimson
still wet against the paper
      she leans in: one, two, three
         rendering the perfect profile of a ballerina
newly emerged,
      the painted dancer
free of her chrysalis,
      toes on point in tiny pink slippers
         twirls around and around
caught in circadian rhythm,
      old as fairy circles danced at midnight,
         trying out graceful limbs
      rippling through space as
one arm slowly reaching
         toward a star,
         gently
      curves in arc above her head
atop the pedestal,
      silhouette in arabesque
Daughter awhirl
      in thorny rose debris

scratches
     her furious pen in a rush
across the open page,
          a poet writing her story,
defiant dancer emerges
scrawled on paper
     prancing forth in words,
          fresh as the cadence of Spring's
first rose-petaled flower,
     so like the painted ballerina

PLAIN

she was plain
she wore uncreased linen
she laid her head aside adversity

    she let sorrows be
    she held moonbeams close as rainwater

        she took a step
            toward incarnation
as she smiled
        transforming

into someone

    beautiful

NIGHT QUESTIONS

The rich soil of memory
comes up red earth
here in the South

A quiet mist covers the sky
at night making it wet
and mysterious

The questions
I ask the stars
come to me under this blanket

The black highway snakes
in front of me through
dark night skies

The stillness shattered
by the engine noise
I am driving

Outside myself
inside the car
a voyeur to the simple

Drama of night in
North Carolina wondering
how do I talk to my roots?

MY VOICE

I am the note I strive to reach
       deep inside
Billie Holiday's blues
       pinching, forcing, squeezing
concentricities

pump full throttle
       lap against my breast
in open flowing answer
       "I'm a fool to want you..."

Gathered Cloth

I am a yellow calico dress
       hanging on the line

twisting in the wind
       fluttering in answer

to stiff blue overhauls
       bunched under the clothespin

in the yard next door
       breezy sunshifts

dancing through the air
       gather us together

beneath the altar of
       God's summer sky

FIRST DANCE

Santo & Johnny
        sweet guitar
                close dancing

broad tweed-covered shoulders
the smell of wool against
        a smooth cheek

                        aftershave
clinging close
        in sweat-damp shirt

holding on
for the first time
feet barely moving

to the slow rhythm
                arms unused to holding
                        slightly crushing

but eager

DO CHICKS HAVE WINGS?

This chick walks by this guy...
   he breathes out to her
      in a rush of words
       "Hey baby, come 'ere..!"
his voice pushing,
       insisting,
demanding, cajoling,
       entreating her
"Come on over here...!"
      preening, pressing
      (a voice he thinks is sweetness,
       nothing more...)
"Hey, baby, what you doing..?"
her eyes dagger
     as she draws a sigh through her mouth
all the way to her spleen
she says
"None of your nobody business."
       her shadowed back,
  a criss-cross of angles
pricks the space between them
     as she walks on by...
He hears fluttering, flapping,
     winglike rattlings--
could they be doubts?
(white noise from his unsure heart
       poised, ready for flight..?)
Something lacy whooshes
     above his shoulders,
as he ducks...
his thoughts roll over
     and pop in cartoon bubbles
beside his head,

She did what to me?
                    Rushed on by?
This   guy picks up his smile
dusts it off
                and wonders...
Do chicks have wings?
        Or do I?

Deep Sky

Oh, bring your deep sky back
      and let me sprinkle it
with stars

if you hold the blanket
      I'll fetch the cups
together we'll drink early evening dew

there now, let me incline my head
      in the recesses of your shoulder
and as the cloth of your shirt
      creases my cheek

the loosed longing etches my face
      in a pattern of grasses
as old as the hills

when we sit with our knees touching
      just barely
the Spirit fills my head with day dreams
      my heart with hopes

our great will prunes those wild nettles
      into silhouettes
my fingertips a-prick with blood
      from the effort

as your sweet tears quietly pool
      around my hurts
the moment stings just a little
      from the salt

CORNBRED SINGER

She is a cornbred
    singer

pretty voice wafts through
    the air like corn bread
baking in the oven
sweet-smelling
    and just right
alongside a mess o' greens

simple words of love
    longing and loneliness
barely punctuate the
    undulating rhythms of
the music from her mouth

tawny beauty dressed in
    crinoline skirts, hair piled-high
smoothed with Dixie Peach
    stands before the microphone
all innocent and new
    in her seduction

Aleutia sings lead
    Dovey and Purlene back-up
harmonies laugh like sisters
the blend feels warm as liquor
    creamed in hot talent

you can't help but welcome
    the notes into your heart
restin' inside your chest
    close enough to touch your soul

unfretted sounds fill-up
   vibrations multiplyin' like an
egg dividing in the womb
   turns into a sweet child of mercy
whose song spills out to the back row

   This girl is born to it!

BURNIN' WOOD

'fore the mist settles
and the clouds form-up

smell of burnin' wood
fills the night air

the roadways
turn to snakes

and the only lights
stars in the tarry sky

pullin' the
ha'ints out'n

the shadows
near enough to touch

scarin' the Godless
t' nothin' but cinders

HEART-STONES

i found a heart-shaped stone
in my path

turned and picked it up
almost decided to pass it by

adding it to my collection
little heart stones

given to me
by my sons

today i remember
those sweet gifts

and am reminded
of their

childhood

HONEYSUCKLE

cups of honey draught
sweet to my taste
spills in little creamy blossoms
running down my front
making the past I had reached
something to do
with the matter at hand

the whole leafy arrangement
possessing steep and bottom
in the place where
hardness of work disappears
as unlanded memories
encase me as scent
in heady rest

alongside the well of my soul
twining tendrils arun with
possibility
new growth
crouch within cosmic change
bringing a laugh
smeared with a tear

making me realize
the flowering vine keeps me
ready and young inside
liquefied as bee nectar

SOUTHERN CROSS

Why am I here?
in the Southland, ancestry home
the hidden swath of memory
holds secrets of my being—
a mere ribbon of connection
uncurling
from the sky

I always look
to this unblinking source for answers
and sometimes I find them
crossed
in the reflection of
a buttercup
held under my chin

STONE FRUIT

Roots reach deep along the Rice Coast, in South Carolina, yielding sweet-grass grown for the plaiting of baskets needed to hold grains of rice. Inez Pitts is daughter born to Lance and Dominga, who once lived on the sister coast in the Great Land. The land of Africa. In Sierra Leone, tall palms and cassavas grow fat and complacent as they clutch the earth ripening under father sun, offering fruitful bounty. The ways of the harvest are simple. Planting, the one way of life before the difficulties began. Before the ancestors of Lance and Dominga's journey to the slave yard and the island-in-the-middle-of-the-river, all life was simple. Here on Lady's Island, on the Carolina coast, Inez Pitts spent her childhood. In many ways, it is not so far from the island-in-the-middle-of-the-river, Bunce Island, Sierra Leone. Inez is nicknamed Pitty, from the stone fruit she picked as a child. Orange-gold peaches she reached up and plucked from the branches of the tree, held fruit so soft and sweet to the tongue in summer. She picked more than any one else. Pitty is strong. She is great-great grandchild to those of the slave yard. And like the tightly coiled fanna baskets of her Mende ancestors, Pitty carries memories of her people as old as worry on her broad back.

Slaves, stones of people, once sweat under African stars woven through the same heavens as a child Pitty looked up at living beside the tangled South Carolina coastline. Sometimes Pitty quietly listens to the marsh coast natter of the old ways. She hears within herself the people's song of freedom. Even as a girl—which she has not been for seven decades—Pitty knows the music. Though thick in the middle—Miss Four-by-Four they call her—working in the house of the old white woman she cares for in the three floor brownstone near the lulling smells of Baltimore's shipyards, where on Tuesdays she looks outside and sees a single red hibiscus adorn the ragman's donkey cart, even now, inside the sooty brownstone—more burnt than brown to Pitty—she polishes monogrammed silver candlesticks in the pasty afternoon light, then places them on the parlor table and awaits night's darkness bringing together the two skies, one African one American, where everything is everything and 'How you do?' becomes who you are.

Even now, Pitty sees behind her own eyes and relives her mother's stories of prisoners locked within the termite-spewed red clay walls, knotted chains on hands and feet, staked to the island-in-the-middle-of-the-river. Pitty imagines the grandparents of Dominga and Lance, boxed-in, as they must have been as children, as she hums the same songs, singing of the secret squares of blue sky and the sun's yellow above their African heads. She imagines choosing freedom's bright colors as she sings to herself inside walls of the small darkening apartment.

Pitty takes great care as she places every playing card from the deck in a straight line for her mistress' evening game of Solitaire, joined to the others in the music of the sweet-grass.

FISHERWOMAN'S SHAWL

The Fisherwoman's shawl

                         thrown up

to the sky

          protects the heavens

letting stars

               twinkle through

THE SCHOOLYARD

Brown laces in your brown shoes
      look like they have been dragged
through the puddles inside the school yard

getting your feet wet. While
you are waiting for your son
to come outside for recess.

Usually he is the one
      who drags his feet through puddles,
but today you beat him to it.

Of course, it was really not on purpose
      this dragging of your shoes and laces
through the muddy water.

Of course, you do not really realize
      you did this just like you did
when you were your son's age—

that age when everything you see
      is like a shiny penny.
Maybe that is why

you decide
to meet him at the schoolyard here today

      to share an apple...

JUNE BUG

Along the rutted road she drew in a prayer breath,
releasing it as she swore and bent to untie her tightened shoe.
"Damn this God-foot," she cussed,
"it be a August day and here I am a June!"

"Remember the Grace Period, dear," Juney heard
from the voice from above.

Gnarled branches of a Sycamore by the side of the road
bent that very minute in supplication;
the tree not concerned at all
about the weight of the summer wind,
taking the inconvenience as an event of usual contrition,
no suffrage whatsoever considered in the action.

"Nestles of hayseeds and Buckeye buttons don't make me
the livin' I ought!" Juney spat. "Cain't even get me a proper
set of shoes for these po' pitiful feets!"
"My Lawd what a inconvenience!"

"This is your Lord, and I give you the morning songs of the
Cicadas for your listenin' pleasure. No need to the other. You
just experiencin' a bit of contrariness
in the doldrums is all, Sweet Girl."

"Who that callin' me Girl?
Better yet, who callin' me Sweet?
Cain't be no Lord in this Heaven."

"I do, and I am," said the voice from above,
"and you got Heaven's way with the Scripture today.
What's your pleasure, Matthew, John
or a Psalm?" Juney thought.

"How about the first Should-be Commandment?
The one that goes, Eve tol' Adam to eat the apple,
an' he did is all?
Tha's how it should be anyways—
Eve tellin' Adam, he listenin'.

Only in the Book that old serpent done got in the middle
and ruined Eve's afternoon—
makin' her cry them big ol' tears as she wash, and hem,
an' bend to sweepin' the floor.
They's mans sins if'n you want my opinion."

The voice from above echoed in contemplative response,
"Be charitable, always charitable child—
an Juney, that's bettern' yesterday's tirade
on the vagrancies of male usefulness in The Garden,
is how I think you put it."

Just then that old Sycamore shook as if it had a head cold,
leaves quakin' and branches bowin' down low scratchin' the
earth by Juney's swolled-up feet.
The mitten-like leaves were strainin'
for importance of being noticed
since the start of this morning's impertinence.

Juney looks and says skyward,
"How 'bout given me them leather shoes you has up in your
top drawer, oh Lord above? These canvas ones is wore out.
'Sides, you who you say you are...?
You can spare me a pair of them fine shoes. I like ones with
bright orange laces—kinda' matches my hemline ruffles,
Lord dear."

"Just 'cause it's August and you a June and all,
and the tree grows straight because it's a tree,
and the sun is high and you are prone with debris
from the Fall...tell you what,
I'll make you a new Commandment:
"You have to learn to laugh, it's the way to true love."

"That ain't no Commandment, new or not!
Even I, Juney Harper knows that! Ain't no either or in it.
Am I to suppose the Lord God in Heaven
gets bored with us all down here so he got to make up
Commandments? New Commandment, my feets.
My achin' feets!"

There was just then a crack of thunder and a bolt of lightning
struck across the limpid sky making it seem like night.
Clouds swirled and the leaves from the Sycamore,
the little mitten-like leaves clung to their mother for pure life.
And Juney landed in a heap,
wonderin' if'n she done crossed-over
to the pitiful darkness.

"This is a toilsome time oh Lord in Heaven,"
Juney grumbled out of her pebble-filled mouth.
"Perhaps there is now in my vision
a clear dream to be awarded. I'm a' listenin'," she sighed.

"You like that batten board display, did you?" the Lord
Himself declared.
"You always were a fool for my artistic side.
They'll be no more delusions on a smile
from your God in Heaven.
I think the Sycamore may need some reassurances, though.
You do that for me, Juney?"

39

Juney's thoughts sat smooth for a minute.
She slashed the sky with her look of fire
accepting her dues for the day.
"Thank you Lord above," Juney said all smiles,
and started picking up the dead
branches at the foot of the Sycamore.

The sky returned to its original morning light as
fencerows of possibilities opened themselves before her.
As soon as she bent to her work, all of a sudden,
there under the tree tied to one exposed root
were the orange laces—three hundred of 'em!

Juney looked up and shook her head at the
place in the sky where the voice from above
could be heard and she said,
"Now, what else do you suppose I gotta' do
             for them leather shoes?"

THE PEARL MAKER
(The story of Sojourner Truth)

"Isabella, girl!
    You wash dem clothes right now!
Hurry! Dat Master g'won to beat you if you be slow today,
    go on now," my Mama say.

But I hear more,
    I hear the angels talk to me
through Mama's mouth and they say,
"You be alright child, just listen to
    what Jesus be sayin'. Isabella,
you listenin'?" Mama say. "Just clean
    your ears out now, child,
and listen!" My Mama taught me dat.
An' I been hearin' God's sweet voice from
Jesus' mouth ever since I was a little girl-child.

By the time I be a mama myself and married to a
    slave man old enough to be my pappy,
I birthed five children and had to run.

But I took with me my little infant girl-baby.
    I figure she be needin' the help of the Lord most surely.
I take her and flee dem Masters out into my servitude for pay:
    Tha's Freedom! Sure is.

God done call me Hisself,
He say, "Isabella,
    you take that there pilla' case of you'rn
    stuff it full o' your belongings and follow Me!"
        I followed.
Jesus,
    He be the author and finisher of my faith.*

41

I done heared him ask for me to preach to de others
So I figures I needs God to give me a new name,
                    Sojourner.

I am to be a travelin' pilgrim up and down the land.
                    Truth,
for the people and they sins to see,
        I be a sign to 'em, have mercy!
                            Sojourner Truth.
Anti-slave talk I be sayin' all along,
        the womens need me mo' den ever now.
Womens—Black and White be my cry to prayer!
        We all God's childrun!
        Childrun I speak to God,
and God speaks to me!

He insists, "No man over no woman."
        This be a Godly thing.
        Childrun I speak to God,
and God speaks to me!
                    How I know dis?

I see the ex-slave refugees same as me
in dem muddy camps in Washington livin' Satan's misery,
and I hears God's justice clear as Jesus' sacrifice:
        "Speak Sojourner, be your Truth."

In my own words I speaks for the slaves
        of dark skin color and the fair sex of womens
to all men who think they are of importance,
        so hear me!

"I have plowed and planted
and gathered into barns, and no man could
head me—and ain't I a woman? I have born'd five
childrun and seen 'em mos' all sold off into slavery,
and when I cried out with mother's grief, none but
Jesus heard—ain't I a woman?...
Den dat little man in black dar, he say women
can't have as much rights as man, "cause Christ warn't
a woman.
Whar did your Christ come from?
Whar did your Christ come from!
From God and a woman!
Man
        had nothing   to do

                with Him!"**

Mr. Douglass and the President Mr. Lincoln listens to me,
        I says to 'em, "Is God dead?"

"You a pearl-maker, Sojourner,"
        they two important gentlemen says.

        "We got here the 13th amendment
        to the Constitution of the United
        States of America signed
        and ratified this day,
        December 12, 1865.
        Slavery is abolished!"

"Didn't I say He ain't dead? Mr. Douglass,
        Mr. Lincoln—well, didn't I?"

                ***

This is a recreation of a conversation Sojourner Truth had
with a friend a few days before she died.

Me, old? Yes, I be old,
    it bein' 1883
and my body is plum wore out at eighty-six years.

        What, die?

Well, honey, I'm not gon' die.
I just be goin' Home
        like a shooting

                                star.

                    ***

                    Epitaph***

            Supposin' Truth be a woman?
                What then, Lord?

*Hebrews: 12:22

**From a speech Sojourner Truth gave at a women's rights
meeting in response to men who had spoken with patronizing
solicitude of Women's weakness and consequent
subordination to men. (PCN, Vol. 141 No. 4, All Saints by
Robert Ellsberg)

***Epitaph: This is what I imagine her epitaph could be.

THE LOSS OF REASON

The loss of reason brought me to her house. She was an unoblivious mother, an old friend of a friend told me I should look up. Well I did. She wasn't home. Probably went to the movies. I went in anyway, stepping into the kitchen. And it was true. Everything sighed of core and key without a smidge of loss of regard usually found in such places. (Her house was painted screaming aqua, and inside it reeked of spaghetti-sauce garlic; a purple clove of which lay by the kitchen sink—the garlic, not the sauce. Well, there was a tiny splatter of tomato glued to the counter, but nothing to get the Homemakers Aid Society in an uproar about or anything, besides it was Friday night when I stopped in and folks are allowed a little leeway. Lee and way? Was I having the sailing dream instead? Hard to lee? Or maybe the cow one and way was spelled w-h-e-y? No. That has to be another story. Oh please!)

Anyway, I took a turn up the stairs and inside the bedside table drawer in the guestroom I found a poem written for me. Just me. No other name on it just mine. The pages were crisp and un-opened. Someone had very carefully seen to tying a blue string knotted exactly around the center of the packet—for it was more than a couple of folded sheets, less than a bundle—yes, I'd say a packet of poems. The words struck me in a tug-o'-my-heart sort of way, and when I read them through again and again, no effort of thought slipped up to reason. The poems were beautiful just the way they were. The first was the one about the lonely spider in the barnyard. (Personally, I think someone stole the theme from Charlotte's Web, but maybe not. You know how thoughts can be convergent all at once and in different places, too. There's some anthropological theory in the world that says human beings morphed from one species to another spontaneously on different shores. So there you go. It could be coincidence about the spider and barnyard and all.)

Poem number one:

SPINNING

The sating of appetites
chewed up my thoughts
and I spun one out to you
from the barn door
hoping you would join me

(I'm not sure that's my favorite.)

Poem number two:

BOATS

"The water is wide
I cannot cross over
and neither have I wings
to fly
build me a boat
that can carry two
and both shall row
my love and I"

(Plagiarized. Judy Collins sang that one, but I won't tell. I still like
it.)

Poem number three:

CRASHING

The graphics card
video card
problem monitor
hook up system
crashed...

(Uh! No, that was Thursday's computer nightmare. Brain flip.)

Poem number four:

ROOFTOPS

Rooftops overlooking
pearl bright city lights
keep us cozy in
our languid moments
linking our hearts
to the stars
quiet in the black night

This was the last one. Someone wrote it just for me. I can drop the
parentheses now.

THE COLORS OF SURRENDER

He feasted on
    a string of petit fours
hung 'round my neck,
    and with each bite
the tired spots of
    my life
surrendered

To carmine purpose
    I moved into his quiet
long-stemmed arms
    worthy of humble outlay,
my froward heart still,
    indolent

We became supplicant to dark earthly wonder,
    broth-colored steam
arose from our flanks
    filling empty places with answers
precious as a bowl of yellow roses
    in winter

THE COTTAGE BY THE BEACH

On the stretch of sand ahead of where I stand, a little off the beach path sits the cottage near an out-cropping of razor-edged stalks of dune grass. I know this cottage well, and it knows me. We seem to have grown together. Ours, from the beginning, was romance at first sight. In my mind, I see her history unfold before me. It must be a she, a she of endurance with the look of a plank of driftwood washed ashore. The uneven ridges feel smooth to my fingers, like the ancient hull of an abandoned pirate ship left to bleach in the sun. I sense promises, secrets, on the other side of the old door as I rest my hand on the enameled knob. Quixotic images flit through my thoughts like the discovery of glittery gems hidden in the hold of a vessel. They wink and tantalize. The smell of excitement fills me, and I sense a part of some perfect dream about to unfold.

This is the place I go in my mind where I breathe the smell of salt in the beach air and the late afternoon haze from the shoreline settles briefly on my shoulders. The hot feel of fine sand under my bare feet works its way into my memory and I see the way I want it to be. The sand always feels soft and inviting. I stop and wiggle my toes in a little deeper, reaching for the coolness where the layer just under the surface lingers beneath the hot mid-day burn. I cannot resist doing this. The fine sand, once bits of gritty stone water-smoothed over time, takes my imprint preserving the moment on this spit of beach.

The cottage has withstood much from life's bastard attentions. Hurricane winds whipped from the sea, bent to nature's cruel reason have pounded her frame season after season turning the honed driftwood to silver. Brown sun-burnt shingles, flimsy as a lover's promise, are wind-ripped in places from her rooftop leaving vacancies for rain to pour through. Today, though, she sits quiet, the sun the only intruder, glancing through perfect white clouds. Under the cottage windows pink hollyhocks and lavender bee-balm sway in some previously arranged rhythms. Little yellow and coral beach pebbles interrupted by shards of glazed blue muscle shells and white-encircled clamshell speckle the mortar running up to meet the gray siding. An occasional bit of mica glints through, catching reflections of a lazy butterfly fooled by the cottage's mirrored charm. The butterfly lingers before reluctantly heading toward a more productive visit to a cache of pollen-limned crimson sage growing nearby.

Above, the clouds lean freely into their contrary nature. They form and reform in an unending performance like a circus act along lazy, invisible lines of horizon promising rain one moment, sun the next. Clouds are so often contrary above this patch of beach, whisking away from the shoreline in hurried drags across the crests of waves then back again toward the shifting sky. The sun eagerly gets involved. Sun-glints hit and miss the new born waves and converging sky like dance partners learning their routine for the first time. The sunlight gets caught in the groove between this sea-and-sky world somehow reassuring me my place in it all.

Inside the cottage, yellow walls the color of a remembered sunrise dapple in mid-morning's yawn. Gray-brown ceiling beams reach all the way to the top of the supporting roof tendons. Directly below random width pine flooring, dulled to a soft gleam from years of patterns made by barefoot travelers, stretches from one side of the room to the other. Jeweled rugs of shredded rag crafted into small squares and rectangles lie quietly, show-casing someone else's toil. Smiles and tears seem worked through every weaving, offering a sense of homey comfort on cloudy days to a grateful traveler. Looking across the room I see a monumental fireplace covering the entire north wall. Large gray stones, gigantic magnifications of the grains of sand I worked my toes through moments earlier, run from floor to ceiling. On one of the stones near the top of the driftwood mantle my initials, BAB, are carved. The letters are hardly noticeable, looking almost like they belong there etched by the hand of the waves heard just outside the door. The fireplace is cold. No flames spill warmth from behind the hearth today. Instead the fire screen is hung with a basket of summer wildflowers. Fires in the hearth will come later, when the snow begins to fly and the air turns chill. Today I can just be, still and close, remembering.

Unstrung Pearls

A FONDNESS FOR ORANGES

The little girl, like the poet
     Rilke, has a fondness for oranges

she sits on the hillside
     looking through
the crayon box of colors
in her Honduran cloud forest

as she bites into her orange
     bigger than her whole hand
sweet stickiness
dribbles down her chin

mid-afternoon's welcome taste
     on her hungry tongue

her nostrils tickle
     at spray from the rind
as bitter oil slicks
her nose in quick spurts

keeping secret the luscious
     pulp her palate craves
a minute before the smooth-cased
sacs burst in trickles down her throat

the liquid smells as honeyed
     as the creamy blossoms
small bees burrow in
as they cross-conjugate

on tiny pollen-tipped knees
      nuzzling the nectar
from flower to flower
re-seeding the orange grove

like a band of tiny angels
      hung below gossamer wings
each nodding toward the future of
this black-eyed mountain child

who will never know Rilke's delight
in her perfect being

BEDOUIN BARTERING

A hint of rosewater and myrrh scent the air
as the Bedouin woman passes,
moving in cadence with the hush of the wind,
her dress skirting the sands of the Sahara
blown black from the hills.

Gold coins and bright orange Asian silk frame
her brown face ripe as a date,
as she walks in stately sway
through the market place toward me.

Her arms jingle with her wares.
"My necklaces are for sale!" she cries,
looking like some exotic desert bloom.
"Amber and Lapis—jewels worn by Cleopatra!"
She looks straight at me.
"How much you pay?"

I glance at the baubles dancing in the heat,
a clutch of change already in my hand
deciding my fate, as I ready for the bargaining.

A smile curls from her poppy-red lips,
"Gems blue as the Lily-of-the-Nile!" she says.
Eyes black as kohl look at me,
"These necklaces are treasures,
once worn by a Queen."

She lays one across my neck.
I turn my head to one side, imagining myself
Nefertiti in relief,
Egyptian beauty bowed-to by her slaves.

"You buy, bring you good luck!" she presses.
Her laugh catches like palm fronds rustling the wind.

"Five dollars! American!" she insists.
I dig deeper in my purse.
"Here is two," I say.
"No, three," she snatches the bills from my fingers.
"Bring you a man for sure!"

I let go the money,
we make the trade.
As she places the necklace around my throat,
light catches the glass in
rainbows splayed under my chin.

My eyes look across the winded sand and I see admirers
in the shadow of every turn...

SHE KALLIOPE

Her fractured heart
      spins in confetti
swirls from the sky
         downward
     alights on heads
and tree-tops

pieces together
     a new she
         who knows
no plain cloth
no anticipation
         nothing but
unbolted yardage

sewn together
bit by bit
     re-worked through
     hands set free
creating soul-patches

     wardens of sanity
needled together
     with threads of steel
at last

     out in the meadow of
living
     dreams
airing
     mossy scale
cleansed

          through soft winds
          of encouragement

icy howl of previous
          histories
                         abandoned
     to Kalliope's
               even-song

MY HAT

I left my hat on the chair,
        and as I cross the room
he says,
        "Don't you want your hat?"

there it sits in a flop
        I think
my hat? do I want my hat?

what I want is his face
        in my hand and his
fingers on my back
        rubbing at that spot

where sore muscles need kneading
        and the strings
underneath might sing
        with the right touch

what I want is his voice
        close to my ear
buzzing aloud with incessant
        bee-talk

what I want is his eyes
        to whisper back
in a look as blue as mine
        liquid soul
searchings

where indistinguishable
        mumble nonsense
flutter-wing inanities

reach beyond simple words

what I want is his yearny
      hesitation to quiver
loosening the bends in the river
between us so we can meet
      like this again

instead I look at the chair
      and the hat
and answer,

"My hat?
      Well, sure I want my hat!"

as I place it on my head
      for one small moment
I imagine he knows all about me

THE SUNSET CLUB

end of day light
lowers herself

deep in the morass
of evening's yearnings

spreading indigo
violet and heavy
corals over

the lip of the horizon
sealing in hope
for the morrow's

play—staged
already in the wings

ruffling her sunset skirts
drawing the traveler
across nighttime's trench

allowing heaven's footlights
to spark

and glow behind
pulling down
from above

illuminating each
shadowed face
teasing for a smile

as she slips
beyond grasp
hinting at lively

yellows yet
to come

WHAT SHE HEARD

I believe in music,
> *I believe in love...**
*Mac Davis

So, a ruffle-shirted Stetson riverboats right over
> next to me and drops anchor.

> > "Compassion is a frail thing."

I hear the angels sing,
> but ignore it.
Sweet-like and true,
> eyes wide as the queen of spades,
Riverboat says, "Howdy ma'am.
Sure is a fine evenin,' care to take a stroll?"

> > "Sugar cubes fallin' in a well."

The angels warn.
"I know it. I know it," I say back.
"I been there, I know it! But his
eyes, they're so..."
> > "Black."

The angels mutter.
"He's talkin' 'bout his daddy, hush now," I say.
Riverboat says, "...an my daddy, he left this
here gold purchase just for me.
(He fished his pocket and
drug out a nugget.)
> > "Looks like Fool's Gold from here."

The angels squawk,
tisking their wings in impatient flap.
"Conrad True, Ma'am," he says,
and tips his hat.
"At your service," and he bows.

                    "Conrad True?!! Service to what!!"

The angels are throwing-up now.
I just ignore those pesky angels
and duck under the awning.
"Why, Mr. True," I say, "I'd be pleased to take
your arm and walk awhile."

                    The angels have plumb tuckered
                    themselves out.

I reached my hand out to Mr. True,
and that was forty years ago.
Those angels?
They singin' for Sister Hennesey, now.

An' I think she's listenin'—
only sad thing is, I hear she's still
waitin' for her riverboat
to come along.

HEAVY

Something you don't ever forget is
the weight of your Daddy's coffin,
or the sweat going into
holding it straight before the drop.

I can look back and
see that weight
heavy as a miner's sorrow.

I watched as the six men—
virile young men still
indifferent to years—
haul that casket to its final resting spot.

Barely a bead broke
on any one forehead,
not much armpit heat either
on those young men.
Youth, pure youth!

Way different from
the cold clay of the man—
once my daddy—
resting inside the lined box.

Slabbed death cold as marble
now coffined in bed
for all time
inclined toward questions
sung low as the man's passing.

Honduran mahogany
no cheap pine here—

no sir—
cased the pink velvet
soft and cozy as a baby's cheek
next to his face.

I was girl then,
not woman yet—
yet almost—
but still a girl
young enough to make the mistake.

The mistake?
This girl touched that branch of a hand
sticking out the gray-dark suit—
to give comfort? To the dead? Perhaps.
Instead I felt the cold clamp of eternity
stretching the distance.

Yet as the lid closed
on that gleaming box
the reach between father and daughter
warmed
in the light of an angel
bright as hope
perched atop the coffin.

Looking back today
as woman I know
what the girl didn't quite see—
buried alongside the father
lies the heart of me
in the man I loved to call
                          Daddy.

THIMBLEBERRIES

Thimbleberries...

are sweet juicy memory

    of that long-ago summer

when Grandpa   lay down

    for twenty minutes

after supping the unknown fruit,

waiting for a sign

    of gravity's stillness.

        Hooray! Hooray!

He found the plumped seeds

    innocent fare and in

responsible grace called, "Come back!"

    Pail in hand to join in the picking

as we all swallowed

    the purple berries gobbled up like pie—

Robins watched from the branches.

THE SILVER NECKLACE

the silver necklace
      sends bright boxes
of light

      into heaven's cosmos
      twinkling
mirrored laughter

      courting angels
in their playground
      hanging in strands

      around my neck

THE LADY WHELK

The tip of the lady whelk lies empty
at the edge of the shoreline,
the inside of the shell glistens, slippery with promise
like the inside of a woman ready for love.

Spirals of ocean current constrict and release in rhythm
around her creamy convolutions,
as pinks and corals wet with anticipation
before giving in to the pleasures of the surf.

Soon a new inhabitant crawls inside to make his home,
Hermit-crabbing himself into the shell's vacant corners
prepared to discard her at moments' notice.

The beautiful whelk,
        wiser than that.

VIOLETS FOR MY FACE

The day he brought me violets for my face
      the sky was filled with soot and snow,
icy flakes touched the tip of my tongue
      5th Avenue lights brightened the air
      that snowy February afternoon.

Steam heat sizzled inside the diner
      wrapping me in hamburger smells,
      burger and bun hauled on plates
pulled by the choo-choo train server
taking me my birthday lunch,
      chocolate shake on board!

Eleven is a fine age! I believe completely!
The miracle dressed in gray flannel suit,
      my dad, my hero,
makes violets appear in snow banks,
      fistfuls just for me!!

All he asks is my pixie-pleased face,
      February's flower alight with giggles,
ready to romp
      through winter's fingers,
          Spring always just around the corner.

JINGLE SHELLS

Jingle shells line the shore
        strung in a necklace
left by the tides

they twinkle orange and
        yellow in the Monday sun
catching the eye
        of small children

whose little fingers reach for
        the baubles as if they
were still something valuable to trade

IT'S TIME

If you think about it
        and who doesn't?
It's time for peace.

Didn't John Lennon
        sing to us,
"Give peace a chance?"

Didn't we decide as a nation
        "Life, liberty,
and the pursuit of happiness
        is important?

Didn't we learn in Sunday school
        to "Love thy neighbor?"
So, what's the issue?

Reach your hand over the fence
        and touch my fingers.
I will reach over the next fence
        and touch my neighbors'.

You see how it goes.

LACEWORK

white folds, simple gauze cloth
      wrap the songs
of childhood
enfold contours

a mother's wisdom bears
      her baby's genius
touches

      indiscriminate ripples
a mark in yellow
      crayon moments

seen through her
      lowered black lashes

LIKE HONEY

In my dream of you
you move like honey
through my hours

sticking to my senses
in free-flowing connection
slow and sure

pooling in and around
my secret places
warming my smile

at the hearth of your generous spirit
cozy as Christmas flannel
soft next to my skin

soaked in yellow comfort
exquisite as rose petals
and as full

PAINTED HANDS

(Study on the oil painting: *Nonchalois*
by John Singer Sargent)

every stroke of the oil laden brush
blots the painter's canvas with questions
capturing secrets of life held within,
each curve and flush of color
bleeding through the pigment
fleshing out the young sleeping woman
silhouette shapely as the light at dusk
yearning for things beyond reach,
brush traveling hurriedly down the face
nose pert with nostrils slightly flared in sleep—a warning?
revelation?
roughed lips emerge unparted in unconscious decision
her core incompletely drawn in strokes broad and chopped
clear to the observant,
scent imagined like an awakening rose within
aside the unlined luminescent cheek
aglow in nature's gift of youth,
soft not-yet-determined chin curving
down to her black beribboned throat
dreaming of a necklace of pearls being strung
along her neck sure as dew on a spider's web at dawn,
bushes of her hair lie brushed back against the pillow
in dark, thick luxurious waves covering entirely
her ears and framing her face,
the girl sleeps on the summer sofa
draped beneath creases of dull gold cloth
the suggestion of bosom underneath,
a paisley print shawl belonging to her aunt sprawls
across her lap having slipped from her shoulders,
hidden from view are her feet perhaps bare

tucked beneath the puffed skirt of stylish green gown,
her hands basking in late afternoon repose
contours of flesh, bone and muscle
lie idle, resting loosely clasped on her lap
tapered fingers blushed the color of innocence
loved for what they are,
satisfied beauty not yet complete

MY FUNERAL SILK

I spent the afternoon unraveling my funeral silk
    checking for holes within the
careful quiltings and nattered threads,
      woven beginnings collected strand by strand

Gently my fingers coddle and soothe nervous fabric
    once bound to disorderly flesh gowned in reddest red
eagerly testing truth in the back seat of the Dodge
    strengthening the burn

Smeared hands pull the gathered hempen cord into
    elegant refinements filling-out shouldered places
searching pockets for heirloom pearls,
    tiny worlds of creamy white, pure as Mary's sorrows
needled in and around the folds of wedding lace

Weary thumbs press fond rememberings
    next season's unstrained swellings
quickened under cradled births,
    told in bib-stories,
cross-stitched bunnies and leggy fawns
    nibbling even spaces between nights and days of
childhood's darling hour

Couched in sweaty palms threads bunch and
    spindle into blood stains, torn out love-work
coffined in appliquéd finery ragging the hem line,
    rotting fibers sunk in sad places

My thimbled fingers gather piece-work
graced by evening's tear, drop-stitched seductions,
French-knots worked loose
    gradually slipped into

a blue sheltering shawl

> Deliberately my knowing fingertips take up the work,
pull the one free thread
> left trailing,
unbound silk,
> waiting patiently for heaven's
>> satined joinery

MOONSCAPE

Hope hangs in the sky as
    Queen Moon nestles between
the winter trees lying
    in shadows below

Like a coveted silver coin
    she shines
in her early evening outfit
    lighting the road before her
smiling as she goes

The still sphere
    heaven born
pans over me
    as I watch her—
sister—possibilities uncurl

Like a ribbon
    of quiet diamonds
weaving hearts
    together
preparing for nighttime guidance

The hour not quite there yet...

LUNCH FOR THE ANTS

A bit of green apple
    fell straight from my mouth

I watched as it traveled and landed due South
    on the sand by the shore

I thought with a laugh
    lunch for the ants! 'Twill be evermore

The waves pounding and
    singing their seafaring song
rhythmically moving the minutes along
    gay as a sailor at dusk and at dawn

It wasn't but two when the cavalcade started
    the apple turned brown, tho' sweet, it was rotted

The ants didn't care—for once neither did I!
    To escape the strewn pathway I encountered the sky

Against the clouds sheer delight
    I sat cloaked in favor
sun burning so bright

Lizards and Leopards

When lizards and leopards run 'round the room,

    I chase them in circles with my long corn broom.

Sometimes they laugh and sometimes they squeal,

    but oh how silly they look when they do

    the Virginia Reel!

You may think it's certain, and I know it's quite true,

    that lizards and leopards would rather run free,

than be shoes or fur purses for you and for me.

GRAY AND RED

gray light cringes at the lip of the sill
seeping through the room where
my mother sits in her chair

>	the chair says it all: wheels chrome, handles black,
>	seat blanket-covered

her hair white on her head
(the essence of gray)

her crimson-painted lips curved downward as
TV drones in the corner
marking time

>	above the back of her head hangs
>	the canvas she painted in 1989:
>	Polo ponies, riders with mallets in mid-swing,
>	one player's red-jacketed arm reaches close to earth
>	skirting the ground, his shoulder leans into the hit

the brush strokes shout, "I can take you!"

>	lively sunset corals and burgundies ride through
>	my mother's evening window
>	filling her room with warmth,
>	she looks out, a triumph of sorts,

"Every room should have a little red in it."

>	she says to no one in particular

GODDESS THERAPY

The Goddess of catastrophe
    visited me yesterday.

She twitched her serenity
    into a harpoon

lancing my fragile sanity,
    cackling as she withdrew

common sense.

Purifying the thread and needle,
    she left me alone to stitch myself

back together.

My needlework
    ready to line a Robin's nest,

or a chance raveling in Persephone's Springtime dream.

Her fated Sister swirled briefly before

    my eyes, satisfied, disappearing completely

into a dust mote.

    Why…I could vacuum that girl right back to eternity,

you know?

DESCENSION

descend into poetry
    of wakened moments

bring subconscious
    slings out for meetin'

court the spark despair
    leaves on the pillow

mumblings turned
    full company

production of being
    blotting weariness

onto pointy heads
    and watch derision

mysteriously vanish into
    mid-air release

the lines familiar
    as carved icons

CALIFORNIA LIVING IN THE '90s

Everything here fits in day-tight boxes

     Dale Carnegie style

yet my smile pours out sunshine all around

     the grid

gumming it up

     in Joni Mitchell butterscotch

sticking my heart where my head used to be

     letting me snuggle down in the corners

TUXEDO JUNC-SHUN

I close my eyes
       and see you
seated next to me
       tuxedoed
satin lapels
       pert bowtie
head erect
       your charm
quiet dignity
       intent on the violin
performance...

your profiled silhouette
       unaware
the longing beneath
       my cosseted
sequined gown
       silken throat
       seed pearl
necklace
       clasped around
junk-et-ed thoughts
       dream-secrets
locked behind
       heavy lashes...

THE ROSE POEM

(A Study on Harrison Fisher's Painting:
Lady Reading)

the lady sits poised in the chair, back straight,
left hand to her temple
elbow touching the suggestion of
a writing desk, flat and unadorned

books lie sprawled in front of her
tossed hurriedly, in a heap,
she holds one open to the page
its back propped awkwardly against two others

a long-stemmed white rose with
deep green leaves rests
on top of the stack, momentarily discarded,
like the perfect face of the young lady

who sits there alert and focused
the rose is fresh and open,
the lady is silently reading
from a volume of Emily Dickinson

searching in solitude for the love poem
her young man recited, by memory,
moments ago on their walk
through the library garden

there is no mis-placed hair on her lovely head
nor a look of fidgeted-buttons
along the front of
her wide-collared blouse,

something about her cosseted manner reveals
an earnestness upbringing does not require,
something deeper appears on her brow
as she trains her eye on the printed page

a pinkish hue
blushes her soft, soft cheek
only a little
for others who take any notice...

GREEN AND YELLOW
(A Study of Picasso's Painting: *Girl Reading*)

there's green,
               then there's yellow,
         and the green is
chartreuse
              this color is not really—but almost

      artifice

instead it seems closer to the color of early moss
         announcing Spring

the artist's line dashes into the
              silhouette of a girl seated,
        legs crossed
at the table with a book
        she is reading

the book does not lie open
         on the tabletop but,
is propped at an angle beneath her eyes
        making it necessary
for her hands to hold the spine upright

her head bends intent
        over the printed pages
which she flips quickly,

        one can see,

the girl's yellow hair
        flows over her shoulder
making a space,

a private world
holy
        as the inside of a tiny chapel

Picasso's brush strokes slather
        purplish-brown, puce;

a thick desktop emerges
        where the girl's elbows sink onto the surface
holding the weight

his painter's line drops away again
        to her legs and feet,
a suggestion of schoolgirl shoes
        under the table

        as daylight slides through

                the strands of her thick yellow hair

THE MEANING OF LIFE

Yesterday I inhaled the moon,
    chewed up the stars,
spit out the sun,
    and waited for the meaning of life
to hit me.

An hour went by.

Ants crawled on the lid of the empty Coke can,
    leaves quivered on the Birch
in the afternoon breeze;
    rain began to drip on the evening
newspaper on the sidewalk,
    and the 8:13 stopped at the bus stop

Smackeroo! Right on time.
I scratched my head and sighed.

I decided to wash the pomegranate seeds
    one-by-one,
make a banana cream pie—
    but first cut out the brown spots
on the bananas—
    dust the kitchen table with a rag
and some kind of ammonia spray,
    open the oven door to see if it needed cleaning.
It did, so I closed it.

Outside, the Mockingbirds complained,
    the neighborhood dogs barked,
my black Lab even chased his tail
    in circles around the living room floor,
while lawn mowers down the street

buzzed grass into a half inch carpet.

Finally, I got drowsy and nodded off.

That very night the moon, round and full,
        glowed soft above the apple tree.
And in the morning the sun rose
        fingering a freshened Venus
in his clever coral make-up.

The stars started fading to day
        neatly tucked in
their constellations,
        sleepy in the sunshine—
                all but one bright star in Orion's belt.

I swear

                someone

                        took

a bite

        out of it.

THE HARVEST

Milo, cotton, corn and tobacco fields
line back roads
here in the heart of North Carolina

fall bounty a necessity
an allowance of nature's harvest
nattering from barely stilled tongues

stories of human dignities
fought
recently won

as quiet breeze
rustles through hollow stalks
remindings of yesterday's tears

ROSA ON THE BUS
A tribute to Rosa Parks, Civil Rights' Leader

Rosa smiles
cheeks tawny with pride
her mouth a crease in determination:
Rosa Parks.
Rosaparks, Rosaparks, Rosaparks
herself in a seat
on the salty side of the bus
pepper unhidden.

Blackn'white, blackn'white, blackn'white
salt and pepper buses
drive through town,
stopping for riders.
Step in the front door
two dimes fare
get out and walk—no run!
to the back door to find a seat.

"Sometimes you get left
in the dust
the fare you just paid
is on the bus."
Ten seats white
ten seats in front
thirty-six seats in all.

White blots of passengers climb
on board
dark heads bow in suffered rage
day-laborers pushed together
burdened
hats held in hand

lacy handkerchiefs dab at sweat-worked brows
on stuffed-out cushions
crowded
in the back.

Saltn'pepper, saltn'pepper, saltn'pepper
sprinkled together,
fool Sojourner's ghost
glassy through the dirt-streaked bus window.
Another stop,
Montgomery's Court Square.
Auction spot for slaves
echoing
Colored to the rear,
exhaust fumes choke riders
dark as African truth.

Bus driver says,
"Let me have those seats!"
Three shaded men rise,
Yessuh take my seat, yessuh take, yessuh...
But not Rosa.
Rosa Parks.

Rosaparks, Rosaparks, Rosaparks
in the white section
stretched to eternity.
A word from the driver demands,
"Make it light on yourself, now..."

With a smile
Sweet-as-the-rose-at-the-foot-of-Mary,
Rosa says:
"Do what you want, I'm not moving."

PEGASUS

Haste makes me nervous,
    buzzing around my head
like unsatisfied bumblebees
        giggling
at the edges of the wind
    asking me
where I'm going every minute
    wasting
precious moments at the kitchen sink
    washing
the pomegranate seeds
            one-by-one...
Cracks
            in my thoughts
    give me
            quick
looks of my uncle
    sailing his Pegasus
            cleanly, smoothly, silently
on top of the salt-crusted
            waves

A WOMAN WITH SOFT HANDS

A woman with soft hands
    bid me God's blessing
as our palms touched
    I dropped my loose change into hers

In silence, she told me
    of the sorrow
her brown skin endures

The bending and the towing
    just the weight of it
weeped through her eyes
    the color of tobacco leaves

She didn't smile
    sharing for a moment
her great heartache
    the strong pulse beneath that
careworn touch in her fingers
    dissolved my whiteness

My privilege fell away
    in God's instant
to something greater
    than the hot touch of cultures

Briefly we gave birth
    to understanding

SUGAR GIRL !

Sugar Girl?

You go 'way from that window now
        Get back to your cake bakin' and
Finger dipping into the frosting bowl

Go ahead and swirl up them chocolate fudge and
        Sweet praline cupcakes
Just waitin' to pop in the oven

Little somethin' I can give your sour sisters
        To fight over!
They ain't no candy canes, them two—
        They's more like shot silver drops
All hard and tasteless

(A body could break a tooth
bitein' into one o' them atop a frosted cake)

I'm tellin' you this portion
        So get on back to that bowl Sugar Girl
With the wooden spoon in it

Now stir!

Or all them trees outside is gonna
        Turn to icing and melt the sky over
        like stick taffy
while you been starin' at it

All this rippling joy out here
        'cause of your determined apple pie self

Good-ness Girl!

What is I
      your Godmother
to do with my wand
      on a precious
Lump o'Sugar Girl like you?

VILLAGE WOMAN

you are proud
> yet you are humble

you are perfect
> yet you are chaste imperfection

evolving
> ever-changing soul woman

clothed in green
> growing, bending

molding adversity
> into fortune

sometimes playing with
> the very clay

of creation

THE KEYS TO PARADISE

The best thing about a tropical paradise is the water. The next is the soft fine-grained sand. My husband, Bill, and I found ourselves enjoying both on the island of Maui for a week's vacation we treated ourselves to after twenty-five years of marriage. Five minutes after our arrival we wondered why we'd waited so long. The air was perfumed with fragrant plumeria blossoms and the skies were the clearest blue I've ever seen. It was a real tropical paradise.

Our days drifted. We swam in the condo's miniscule swimming pool (11 feet wide by 15 feet long), I spent a panicked morning in a Longs Drug Store babbling at the pharmacist about how to extract sea urchin quills from my left kneecap, and Bill spent one whole afternoon in the hospital emergency room having bits of coral surgically removed from his eye. Even so, it was a great week. We visited Maui's only winery and sipped pineapple wine one breezy day, and snorkeled most afternoon's away in the deep water off a dive boat by Molokini Crater.

The snorkeling was by far my most favorite tropical activity. However, I only used the enticing little baggies of fish food the first time out. Tucked just inside the elastic leg opening on my bathing suit, the bio-degradable equivalent of doggie biscuits for fish, was in place for feeding. The fish guidebook promised, "Colorful fish will surround you and eagerly look for food." They sure did. A school of hungry silver-grey tropical minnows (I looked them up later on my fish identification card) nibbled and bit until my leg looked like I had spent the day in a poison ivy patch. Red welts were left by fish who obviously hadn't learned to sit up or rollover for their packaged treat.

After the fish-feeding experience, lolling on the beach gazing at the tropical waves sounded good. So, next morning Bill and I walked across to the beach to spend time soaking up rays. In a few minutes, trouble: no bathroom. Being a woman who lives by the principle "if you see one, use it," I improvised. I limited liquid intake—that made me dehydrated, yet strangely full at the same time. The waves, I was sure, held the answer. If I really had to go to the bathroom, well…

The waves started at four feet in height. I decided to go for it. The first three goes were a charm. I dived in and as the wave crested, my head and shoulders popped up and I propelled myself back to the shoreline—piece of cake. My husband was happily sitting under a cocoanut palm ignoring signs to "watch for falling fruit" engrossed in his newly purchased paperback. Bill never read anything but *Airplane Modeler* and *Science Today* at home. Somehow Tom Clancey's plot-driven, action-filled spy thriller *The Hunt for Red October* changed all that. Bill hunkered down under his cocoanut palm and stayed glued.

Meanwhile my fourth wave-ride was coming up. As before, I dove in. As thoughts of how wonderful this tropic paradise truly was skittered across my mind, my arms pulled deeper under the water. A minute went by, my arms flailed recklessly, and my head bobbed briefly to the surface. I barely got a breath in as I spluttered for help before another wave pulled me out further. This time I used all my strength pulling on the diagonal, finally bursting through just before the wave spit me out on the shoreline. I landed in an unceremonious heap, gasping, my bathing suit twisted almost backwards. Every strand of my hair was coated with heavy wet sand, I smelled like day-old seaweed.

Panting in front of Bill a moment later I said, "Good book?"

"Yeah, this is the…what happened to your hair?" He answered.

"I almost drowned!" I shouted with as much dignity as a walking, middle-aged mermaid could muster. Then I cried.

After my well-earned nap, Bill announced, "I have tickets to the best luau in town." I accepted the peace offering. The luau was spectacular—right down to the blue drinks with the tiny umbrellas in them. I smiled as memories of our twenty-fifth floated through my head. We'd had our scrapes, but still, what a paradise. Sauntering over to the rented sports coupe, Bill turned and said words I will never forget, "Got the keys?"

STANSFIELD STANSBURY

Stansfield Stansbury lives in a jar,
and eats raspberry tarts just as they are.
He says, "Yes'm and no'm,
and I think it quite so!"

And quotes Dickens and Keats
wherever he goes.
Stansfield Stansbury is a bit of a pose.

He knows mountains
are high and valleys are low;
that fish live in water,
and frogs hate the snow.

He thinks he's quite clever,
witty, and most urbane.
But some think he's stuffy
because of his name.

Stansfield Stansbury's a cricket
you see, with high hat
and tails and a little pet flea.

The flea's name is Milton,
and attached with a leash
is his rhinestone collar
just dazzling to please.

Together they live in a tall mason jar,
pleased as punch to stay
right where they are.

Milton brews moss
'just right' for their tea,
and sweepings and peels from
the old lemon tree.

Nobody knows how clever this flea,
but the jar is just spotless
to look out and see.

For friends passing by
an invitation stays open,
"Do join us for supper,
your comp'nys most welcome!"

So Saturdays and Fridays and
Sundays quite often,
the cricket and flea entertain with abandon.
Their joy and friends' laughter
ring out in the garden.

And make no mistake,
there's standing room only
right up to the sink!
For Stansfield and Milton who must
live in a wink.

All manner of parties are
celebrated this finely,
and no one enjoys this as much as the host;
whose purpose in life includes
a wee more than a boast.

Yes! Stansfield Stansbury does live in a jar,
with Milton his flea and companion so far;
together they've learned that friendship exists

in poetry, tarts, and tea-with-a-twist.

The garden out back holds
one more suggestion for collectors of jars
of canning dimension;

you must come join them on one fine occasion,
or a cricket like this
may vanish to imagination...

Grace O'Sundays

TOUCH HOPE

Put your hand in my hand
    and touch the skin
of brotherhood

Put your smile in my eyes
    and see the soul
in communion

Put your heart at my feet
    and walk the path
of belonging

Put your faith in my being
    and open yourself
to God

I CATCH THE STARS

I catch the stars
in winking wars
across the nighttime's fancy

as windows latch
against cool air
that moves the skies so fairly

then as the moon
peeks through the clouds
at 3 am's bright landing

the treetops shake
no wind abates
until the spirit standing

upon the morn of
paled-out storm stretch
hands held out with envy

those cold-caught stars
hide crouched in jars
touch fingers worn and weary

hearts formed in play
from soft plied clay
bring Eden's face to glory

rough staff to brook
the world's pure look
abounds in Christ's told story

I catch the stars…

GRACE-FULL

the one bowl
holds the universe
the heavens
the stars
the font of Islam
the piercing point of Christianity
contained within
something of glazed elegance
holding batter for sustenance
fuel and thought
rounded gentleness
cradling heartbeats
providing food of the land
drink of wonder
imitating
cupped hands
held high
the receptacle
holding grains of life
vessel of rivers
seep through soil of regeneration
seeded deep in our borderless hearts
chalice to the blood of spirit
filled with grace
for all

MORNING

a little bit of blue

    in the white

altar flowers

    beckoning

me to smell

    morning's freshness

SOLAR PLEXUS

birth comes up every morning

     along with sight

flavoring first moments

     powdered in possibilities

slow emergence of wonder

     glows in recognition

of the one true Being

     felt within

ADAM SLEPT

Adam slept
        while Eve painted her toes
the colors of simple rainbows

She sat surrounded by
        female generations,
he lay there like a crucifix

Praise is comely for the upright
        sings the Good Book
borrowing from her lovely tears

Eve's eyes glittered
        over her trifling loss
caught in heaven's white-gloved hands

Adam yawned
        sending smoking flax
forth to judgment's victory
                confusing nothing

THE HOLLOW OF ANGELS

I brush the hollow
    above my upper lip

and consult with the angel
    who lives there

her wisdom

is mine for only
    a touch...

she whispers her wings
    against my finger

and I hear her sweet
    voice say,

Love
    me
    first,

all else will follow

OVER THE VERGE

Spring looks out along the meadows' rolling verge
  ruffled at the edges with a glad Robin's song

    his crimson vest puffed in pure delight
    encounters morning under sun's fresh yellow light

the worm is caught amongst the brackish surge
  through ant trail kingdoms crossed on dew-splashed lawn

    as leaves of gold fill-out each blossom-bending branch
    catch the breeze in gusts atop the craggy hillcrest stance

butterflies and birds afield engage the thrill of nature's word
  splendid in freedoms' play through daytime's hour gone

    when cool shadows lean toward evening's settled station
    and stars wink true in bedtime's quiet conversation

not once do Spring's small creatures bow
  to owning sins of scarlet night

or know the pain in Eve's pure heart
  on her soft soul's predestined plight

MY GARDEN GROWS

I see the sky on summer's night
cast shadows drawn against the light

from day's hard toil under heaven's blue
lies new mown lawn now wet with dew

the shifting clouds above tall trees
brings all of nature to her knees

and when I close my eyes to rest
the garden grows her earthly best

curled at night each blossom's beauty
opens wide as sun wakes to duty

refreshed and ready for the day
I clasp my hands first, then pray

MARY'S THORNS

Mary wraps the blue cloth around her shoulders;
the one God gave her.
    She feels the scratch of the weave
through the softness of her struggling soul
      trying to lay hold on eternal life.

Clinging close to a mother's marrow
    Mary weeps everlasting tears;
her familiar comfort.
    Openly they fall deep upon her blue bosom,
the very gown heavy with sorrow.

Is He hers—this thorn-crowned man-child before her?
    His beautiful head bleeding,
the warm blood Mary tastes as her own.
    Removed from her womb was He
truly born to be re-born? This Son?

Her everyday mother's heart
    gone dark with fear, sighs,
as care-worn fingers used to reap and sew
    quietly—tentatively—reach out
to touch just one last precious tear.

The Son's eyes already yoked to heaven,
    open wide to the universe,
strangely adrift from his mother's
    sight.

Below
    the horizon grows fragrant
      with Mary's perfect rose,
    a thorn of faith cradling her mantle.

THE LIQUOR OF THE LILIES

there on the decorated altar
the liquor of the lilies
inebriates my soul
as it drips through
the little of moments
awakening me to the
everlasting corona of truth
crowned in bright pinpricks
on Christ's head as He
touches my being and I
taste the blood of forgiveness
traveling my tongue to the
sanctity of contemplation's birth place
the spot inside my heart
where the Gospel singing begins
buoyed by the honeyed fragrance
released in
full-grown white roses and lilies
nature's perfect allowance
clinging within
my faith's fondest desiring
bringing me to my knees
succored in stillness

EDEN'S GRACE

behold
the challenge

Eden held
when we

were left
alone

PEACE LIKE A RIVER IN MY SOUL

Two days
    amongst the grandeur of
the sage-scented hills
    we pause—

Stop to smell roses
    beneath the rich soil of
spiritual growth
    unlikely roots
woven together
    through memories of
flying fish
    in Osprey talons

Standing alongside
    these satin waters
of silk souls
    we are lured
into the Wilderness
    breathing in ebb and flow
over newness of life
    rest and embrace

Opening to
    God's love
through each
    perfect face

*Written by Ring Lake Centering Prayer Group
July 19, 2002
Edited by Bobbi Dean

WHITE LINEN

White linen
wraps Jesus' body
safe within
the moment
He knows
death
is near
as blood
runs royal
along alabaster arms clean as hope for all the brightness
reflected in beauty crossed between heaven and earth
drawn upon
hard faith
crowned in
a son's mercy
even He
could only
realize inside
heaven's woven
blanket
red-stained
with our
humanity

Iroquois Nation

wooden-stick Creator's game

lacrosse on the hill

CHURCH PAINT

Chips of paint flake into my hand
as I touch the old window sill.
Scrape, scrape, scraping—
layers of yellow history crumble through
my fingers into dust
taking church secrets to the grave.

The tall sashed window groans
in my effort to open it—
now ready for a fresh coat.
Wavery glass as old as steeple brick, older maybe,
looks out onto
the changing world.

The walls inside sigh with conviction,
knowing man's imperfection and toil hold
the edifice built to house prayers.
Hope, grace and everlasting love breathe
through the cloistered goodness
as in fellowship
our brushes dip into the pan.

Bringing up glossy coverage, yellow again,
stroke by stroke working hands
reach and plunge to the task
rooted in the comfort of ritual.
The welcoming walls clothed in gold hue
dry in regal satisfaction.

Warm conversation continues
at home
in the sanctuary.

Only the old window
behind its' new coat
offers
a look beyond.

TAKING THE TIME TO LISTEN

there is a voice I hear
        when I really care to listen
telling me what to say

there is a voice inside me
        getting louder everyday

the words round out
        the verse
deviling the shadow play

there is a voice runs through me
I no longer bend to fear

        it is the one true voice
no longer set apart
        it is the sound of God's
quiet breathing within my grateful heart

RELIQUARY

On normal ground
      just below the surface
            streams of dreams catch the

roots,
      nourishment

feeding the cool-tipped light
covering differences in a veil
      of chosen rivulets

woven,
      as a cloth of faith

protecting the center
      within the whole
of the all and the Magnanimous

      Is that not

           Divine Love..?

THE HUM OF EACH OTHER'S VOICES

The hum of each others' voices
recedes as firefly hour opens
           one last child's game
       played in dappled light
under the branched porch of old tree limbs
           whose leafy arms sing and sigh

Soothed, still, by a mellifluous womb
       playmates laugh
inside this protected place,
     of storybook Angels
     of cradled innocence
unaware the sparks
     about to burst forth
           in Nature's sweet juice

The pals perch on the tip of the limb
       together
     alight childhood's notions
hiding and seeking
       a bit longer
before bright mid-day hands
     tease the leaves of the fruited tree
as they enter   arm in arm
     the Garden of Adams' ancestor

Serpent's slithered dark ground
     beckons a turn
on the bet of an apple
     as one child looks at the other
through the pure chatter of heartbeats

Bound by Love's hum

before time on earth began
        its mark
their eyes
       …hers blue, his earthy brown,
now cry sometimes inside
       the cool and greening place
Eve learns her name in
       the meaning of a blush,
her sweet Adam sees
honeyed skin
       and breaks
a fig leaf from its branch   watching
as sap runs white and sticky,
       rent unto his heart her look

deep as the toss of oceans

BREATHING AGAIN

distraction in the church pew
the choir singing loud

noisy neighbors murmur
I take a deeper bow

then close my eyes in mercy
and find it is enough

to hear the church bells ringing
and feel my knees grow tough

BLESSED ARE THEY

She woke up each morning
    and knew—just knew
playing hide and seek with her
    child was good

She walked about her day
    smiling at the picture of a
finger-painted sun squiggly with rays
    her beautiful baby had created

She greeted her husband at dusk
    by the toolshed door
as he came in from the fields
    covered in dark, honest dirt

She cooked their simple evening meal,
    greens and squash—they loved squash!
feeding her family with what she could,
    washing up when they were through

She kissed the forehead of the sleeping child,
    gathered the rag dolls in her apron,
put away the paints and the paintings
    and sat in her rocker with a cup of tea

Late at night as she looked
    through the canopy of stars
before turning in for bed,
    her heart filled with wonder—

And she knew
    just knew
        she was
  blessed.

Habitat hammers

build children's eager day dreams

through hand-held faith work

MY GRANDMOTHER'S PRAYER BOOK

I have a little prayer book
    that fits right in my hand

It gives me daily missives
    some small and some quite grand

The message always soothes me
    in God's benevolent look

As with the Word I struggle
    to find some small re-birth

The book itself is worn
    and spotted gray with age

As scripture, hymn, and psalm verse
    open to the page

Of days and dates in kindled worth
    the blessings large as stars

In breath as sacred as a friend
    whose memory I have found

The secret strengths my grandmother
    encouraged by the teachings

Are mine to share in reverie
    fingers touching parchment pages

Make ours a sharing of the soul
    with Heaven through the ages

Aspen shimmering

like a flapper in the wind

yellow, green, and gold

ACKNOWLEDGEMENTS

Many of these poems were previously published under my Pen Name: Alden Dean

The Wish: **Pegasus Review**

Uneven Threads: **The Bohemian, Writer's Digest**

Plain, Two Doves, Green and Yellow, The Meaning of Life, Goddess Therapy, Painted Hands: **The Bohemian**

The Lady Whelk: **Sanscrit**

My Hat: **Poetry Now**

Rosa On the Bus: **Artists Embassy International, Ridge Writers Publication**

Picking Tomatoes, Bedouin Bartering, What She Heard: **Artists Embassy International**, and also performed by **Natica Angilly Dancing Poetry Society** in San Francisco's Palace of the Legion of Honor

A Fondness for Oranges: **Pearls of Peace**

Touch Hope: **Pacific Church News, URI Poetry, Pearls of Peace**

The Liquor of the Lilies, White Linen, Reliquary: **Pacific Church News**

Peace Like a River in My Soul: **Ring Lake Ranch Newsletter**, written by Ring Lake Centering Prayer Group, edited by Bobbi Dean

Many fellow poets and friends helped me along the way, encouraging me to create a book. The *Thursday Writers* helped me for many moons. I thank them for hearing my first drafts and eventual poems. I learned to work with words—to get just the right one. They taught me how to really listen. *Natica Angilly's Dancing Poetry Society/Artists International* performed my poem *What She Heard* with perfect humor at *SF'S Palace of the Legion of Honor*. Lots of fun! I want to especially thank John Fox, founder and head of the *Institute for Poetic Medicine*, for encouraging me to express all parts of myself in poetry. I learned to simply "be" while creating a poem. I will forever cherish this gift. I also thank *College of Notre Dame Community Chorus* and *Good Shepherd Church* choir under the direction of Doc Peterman for helping me feel every note of the music we sang with spirit. Singing beautiful words in English, Latin, French, German, Spanish, Italian, Hebrew taught me subtle differences in the reverence of their tones through Spiritual connection. Again, I learned to listen. I have also learned to carve words into haiku through the encouragement of members of the *Syracuse Poster Project* under the direction of Jim Emmons. This has taught me patience and persistence. Lastly thank you to my family who has always said: "You can do it!" And I have.

Bobbi Dean

Made in the USA
Coppell, TX
10 December 2020

44028886R00090